LAWRENCE Title Page

LAWRENCE

Visions of Self — The Memoir

by Lawrence "Law" E. Sturdivant Jr

Lawrence — Copyright

ISBNs

ISBN (Paperback): 979-8-218-64062-0
ISBN (eBook): 979-8-993-5035-9-2
ISBN (Audiobook): 979-8-993-5035-8-5

Edition & Publishing Line

First Edition: 2025
Published by Sovereign Crowns Creative House Publishing LLC
An CrownRoot Press Imprint
A subsidiary of Lawrence E. Sturdivant Jr L.L.C.
New Britain, CT

Credits

Cover and interior design: Lawrence E. Sturdivant Jr, with AI-assisted support
Editorial support: ChatGPT guidance under direction of the author

Contact

Contact: hello@lawsturdivantjr.com
www.LawSturdivantJr.com

Legal Required Line

Library of Congress Control Number (LCCN): 2025923394
Printed in the United States of America

Publisher's Cataloging-in-Publication Data

Publisher's Cataloging-in-Publication Data

Sturdivant, Lawrence E., Jr., 1978-, author
Lawrence: visions of self — the memoir / Lawrence "Law" E. Sturdivant Jr.
New Britain, CT: Sovereign Crowns Creative House Publishing LLC, a wholly
owned subsidary of Lawrence E. Sturdivant Jr L.L.C., 2025.

Identifiers: LCCN: 2025923394 | ISBN: 979-8-218-64062-0 (paperback) | 979-8-
993-5035-9-2 (ebook) | 979-8-993-5035-8-5 (audio)

Subjects: LCSH Sturdivant, Lawrence E., Jr., 1978-. | Self-actualization
(Psychology). | Self-realization. | Happiness. | Divorced people—United States—
Biography. | Divorce—Psychological aspects. | BISAC: BIOGRAPHY &
AUTOBIOGRAPHY / Memoirs

Classification: HQ834 .S88 2025 | 306.89092—dc23

Edited and published in the United States of America.
Visit www.LawSturdivantJr.com | @LawSturdivantJr

Dedication

Dedication

For all of them—

For the ones who chose honest shores, the ones who stayed, the ones who left, and the ones who taught me to leave on time.

For every clean fire that taught me to rise and every quiet water that taught me to float—phoenix and lotus, heat and grace.

For my family and the elders who kept a light on; for the friends who told me the hard truths and handed me clean exits; for strangers who became lighthouses; for the communities that live with courage in view of the mountain and by the water.

For the women who were mirrors, the friends who were oars, and the strangers who were stars—and for the one who slipped two fingers into my open palm, reminding me how presence begins.

And for you, reader—may cadence protect your desire, may your boundaries be mercy, and may your landing be yours.

Acknowledgments

Acknowledgments

Sincere thanks to the readers, lovers, feelers, be-ers, believers, dreamers, conjurers, and alchemists—the ones who keep showing up with open palms and honest breath.

To my incredible daughters, Leila & Ei'Zlee; to my twin sister, LaTanya C. Sturdivant; and to my amazing parents, Larry and Dolores Sturdivant—your steadiness, humor, and grace kept a light on.

To my Waterbury, CT roots; to the edge and hum of Long Island and Brooklyn, NY; to New Britain, CT—where this memoir took shape and became; and to Worcester and Boston, MA, waystations that reminded me how returns can rise.

To truth-telling friends and mentors; to the Water Island community; and to the strangers and spirits who became lighthouses just when the shoreline blurred.

Thank you for choosing this book as a landing page in your journey.

Authors Note

Author's Note

There are seasons in life where reflection becomes more than a practice—it becomes a path. *Lawrence: Visions of Self* was born in that space.
A mirror between endings and beginnings. A study of who I was when I thought I knew myself—and who I became when I allowed my truth to breathe.

Every word in these pages is an echo of that permission. Permission to pause. To observe. To grow beyond performance.
Not as a sermon, not as a spell, but as a sovereign account of a man remembering his own light.

I have written and rewritten this story in many forms—love stories, lessons, losses, awakenings—but this one carries my name because it carries my peace.
The peace that comes when self-awareness meets acceptance. The moment the mirror no longer reflects what you fear, but who you've become.

This is not a guidebook. It's not a how-to or a what-next. It's a conversation between the soul and its shadow. Between love and its reflection.
Between who I was, who I am, and who I continue to become.

Thank you for walking this stretch of the path with me.
The next horizon awaits.

—*Lawrence E. Sturdivant Jr.*

Chapter 1 - Papers & Breath

Chapter 1 — Papers & Breath

Epigraph
I learned to unclench my jaw first, then my life.

The clerk stamps the papers and doesn't look up. A clean thud, a small nod, the sound of ordinary government air. Divorce is apparently most comfortable in fluorescent light—no soundtrack, no priest, no thunder. Just a pen cooling in my hand and the exit door that knows me by the way I push.

Outside, the day is bright and square. The sky doesn't change color because I changed my name back to myself. The street carries on with coffee cups, crosswalks, a siren far away. I place one palm on my chest—four-count inhale, hold for four, exhale for six—and let my ribs confirm that I'm still here. Breath is the first quiet contract I signed today.

At home, the kitchen is the kind of clean that proves someone tried. Citrus wipes. A folded towel. Two bowls stacked like a promise and its echo. I stand long enough to hear the refrigerator hum, a low, familiar chord, the same note that used to soundtrack midnight snacks and whispered plans about "later." Later arrived in manila envelopes.

In the hallway mirror—oval, beveled, a soft blur at the edges—I catch the line of my mouth the way you recognize a road you once took in the dark. I love and wince at the same time. I lift my hand to the glass; the man in the mirror does the same. Neither of us flinches.

> [Handwritten Affirmation: I choose clean love, even when the cleaning burns.]

We didn't fail. We finished. There's a difference. Failure drags; finishing bows. Somewhere between those two verbs sits the man I am, learning to allow endings to be precise instead of dramatic.

I put the ring in a small dish by the sink. It leaves a pale circle on the skin, a soft ghost that will tan away by August. A ring is a sentence; today I added a period. The breath makes room for the period.

Memory arrives like a polite knock.

There was a coffee shop with chairs that wobbled. I steadied one with a folded napkin while she laughed at my need to fix things that never asked me to. We were young enough to confuse hope with blueprint, old enough to know we were doing it. Our hands found each other the way two currents find the same bend in a river—wary at first, then sure. I said we would build a home that hums. She said she would keep a light on in the kitchen. We got good at both.

Desire was honest back then—simple, standing on two feet, asking for water. Desire is still honest now, but its voice has changed. It no longer wants me to contort into the version of myself that offends no one. It wants me present. It wants *discipline* and it wants *desire*—not one choking the other, not one apologizing for the other. It wants the truth without costume.

I walk the apartment and notice what we leave when we leave: a sweater over the chair back, a bobby pin near the baseboard, the light film of two people's lives on a bathroom mirror. I wipe the glass and think about how clarity is less about sharpness and more about permission. What do I permit today? I permit myself to be a man who can love without swallowing himself. I permit tenderness that doesn't perform. I permit lust that tells the truth. I permit grief to pass through without building a shrine.

The sun slips to the other side of the building and sketches a new geometry on the wall—two circles overlap, a vesica piscis of light. In that almond shape, I see the life we shared and the life I'm stepping into, neither erasing the other, both insisting on their own edges. I place my palm inside the overlap and feel the tingle of my own pulse. Two becomes one becomes two again. Not loss—rearrangement.

Years from now, I will remember this as the quiet day. The day I rinsed the cutting board and didn't rush. The day I stood barefoot and unafraid in my living room and counted the birthmarks on my right forearm because they are mine and have always been mine. The day I reheated rice and ate it standing up, salt on my fingers, laughing once at nothing in particular, the kind of laugh that happens when a body sets down a heavy box.

I text her: *Made it home. Thank you for the honesty we found at the end.* I mean it. Ending honestly is its own kind of intimacy.

Night comes with a clean moon—first quarter, a shoulder of light. I leave the blinds half open and lie on my back. The moon lays a small white coin on the ceiling. I imagine the ouroboros, the snake that completes itself by learning where not to bite. I am not a snake, but I am learning completion..

If you asked me what changed, I'd say: my posture. I sit in my life now. I stop bargaining with my breath. I stop selling my spine to the cheapest fear. I stop measuring love by how little of me it requires.

There's a practice I keep returning to: place one hand on heart, one on belly; count the breath; witness the mind; return without scolding. Sensation first, story second. In that order, truth doesn't need to shout.

Tomorrow, or the day with a name that feels like tomorrow, I will pack two boxes—hers and mine. I'll find the picture of us at the waterfall and put it in the middle, between books and tea strainers, not as a trap or a test, but as a record. We stood there once, damp and bright, and it was real. I won't edit the past to justify the present. I want a life that can hold more than one correct sentence at a time.

Before sleep, I whisper the old vow and let it molt. Then I speak a new one, simple and exact:

> [Handwritten Affirmation: I will not abandon myself to be loved, nor abandon love to keep myself.]

The room is so quiet I can hear the clock blink. I choose breath instead of a speech. Inhale four. Hold four. Exhale six. The body says yes. The ceiling coin softens. Somewhere beyond these walls a train announces itself, and I picture sparks under steel—brief light, clean heat, forward.

I turn on my side and feel the pace of my heart even out. I think of an open palm—the symbol I draw sometimes in the margins of my notebooks. Open to receive. Open to release. Not clutching. Not pushing away. Just the brave business of being open.

Sleep comes. Not as a reward. As a friend I finally stopped standing up.

Ritual • Anchor Breath (Day 1)

1. Stand or sit tall. One hand to the heart, one to the belly.
2. Inhale for a count of 4 (through the nose). Feel the belly rise.
3. Hold for 4. Notice the urge to rush.
4. Exhale for 6 (through the mouth). Soften the jaw, tongue, and shoulders.

5. Repeat for 7 rounds. Whisper: *I return to me* on each exhale. *Note:* If you feel lightheaded, shorten the counts and continue gently.

Journal Prompts (Keep it plain, keep it true)

- Where did I abandon myself politely? Where did I stay with myself bravely?
- What part of me is relieved today? What part resists admitting it?
- If love required no performance, how would my body sit right now?
- What is one boundary I can honor without explaining?
- Write one sentence you're willing to believe for the next seven days.

Symbol Inquiry (to reveal later)

- Phoenix: When have you burned by choice, and what did you keep?
- Vesica Piscis: What two truths in your life overlap without canceling each other?
- Open Palm: What are you gripping that wants to become a gift? *(You'll meet these symbols again with deeper stories in later chapters.)*

Chapter 2 - Boxes and Boundaries

Chapter 2 — Boxes & Boundaries

Epigraph
Some choices are shovels. They dig the rest of you out.

Morning finds me with tape between my teeth and a marker uncapped on the counter. Two fresh boxes sit open like small stages. I write the first labels without ceremony: Kitchen — hers. Kitchen — mine. The pen bleeds a little in the corrugation. It looks human. Good.

I sort by three rules:

1. If it belongs more to her story than mine, it goes to her.
2. If I bought it to be someone I'm not, it goes out.
3. If it speaks and it's quiet, I listen again.

Measuring cups nest inside each other like parentheses around a life. I keep the metal set that has my fingerprints on it and slide the copper set—hers—into her box, wrapped in the dish towel with peaches on it. The towel is softer than I remember. Some softness travels.

I find the photo from the waterfall and lay it in the center of the box between books and a tea strainer. Not a trap. Not a test. A record. We stood there once, damp and bright, and it was real. I won't edit the past to justify the present. That vow has weight; it steadies my hands.

Texting is simple today:
— *Her:* "On my way at 3. Anything heavy?"
— *Me:* "Mostly books. I'll carry them down."
There are worse endings than exact ones.

A sweater over the chair still holds her winter. I press my nose to the shoulder and inhale the idea of her, then set it in her box without dramatics. Sentiment is welcome; theater is not. My breath keeps time—four in, four hold, six out—until the urge to keep what isn't mine loosens.

The marker squeaks across cardboard: Keep. Donate. Return. The *Return* pile surprises me—objects that are perfectly fine but not faithful. A chemex I wanted to be the man who used. A set of linen napkins that made weeknights feel staged. Admiring a life I didn't live kept me from living the one that fits. Today is a fitting day.

Inside the bathroom cabinet a bobby pin waits at the lip like punctuation. I leave it on top of her box, visible. We did many things wrong and this right thing—clarity—won't be hidden.

By noon, the apartment sounds new in its echo. The refrigerator hum has more room around it. I hear the building settle, a slow creak that reminds me nothing collapses all at once; it loosens, then chooses.

She arrives at three with a calm face and careful shoes. We move like workers, which we are. I carry books; she carries the small, precise things—jewelry dish, travel comb, the candle that smells like clean rain. We don't pretend we are strangers. We don't perform being fine. We place what belongs with where it belongs.

At the door she looks once around the room. Not a scan, a blessing. I match it. We exchange a quiet thank you that covers more ground than it sounds like. When the elevator doors close, I let my shoulders drop two inches. Weight leaves in odd measurements.

I re-walk the rooms with a slow eye and find what remains: the good chair, the plant that refuses to dramatize light, a bowl with three limes. I stack the empty boxes flat, lean them against the wall, and write one more label: Next.

[Handwritten Affirmation: I sort to honor, not to punish.]

I make rice. The small hiss of the pot is proof that ordinary life continues to vote for itself. When I eat, I stand at the counter, salt on my fingers, and it feels like telling the truth with my posture. Tonight, I'll move the bed six inches to the left so the morning light finds me clean. Small edits; big difference.

This is what boundaries feel like in the body: not a wall, but a corridor. Long enough to walk yourself through.

Ritual • The Box Practice (Day 2)

1. Set a 25-minute timer. Choose one zone (drawer, shelf, surface).
2. Make three piles: Keep / Donate / Return. No "Maybe" pile.
3. Breath cadence 4–4–6 the entire time; shoulders soft.
4. When the timer ends, bag Donate, stage Return, put Keep away.
5. Step outside for 90 seconds of natural light; say (quietly): *Exact is kind.*

Journal Prompts

- Which objects tried to make me someone I'm not? What do I return because I respect both of us?
- Where did I feel a clutch in the body—throat, chest, gut—when deciding? What was the sentence underneath it?

- Write one paragraph that starts: *We didn't fail. We finished. Today that means...*
- What can I move six inches to the left in my life that would change the light?

Symbol Thread

- Open Palm (appears in margins this chapter): the discipline to release without flinging, to keep without clenching.
- Vesica Piscis returns in the layout of the two boxes—overlap honored; edges respected.

Chapter 3 - Ash & Architecture

Chapter 3 — Ash & Architecture

Epigraph
Some endings are kilns—they harden you into a use.

The morning is brisk enough to make the window honest. I crack it, let the cool thin air slip in, and set a small steel bowl in the sink. The bowl has seen pasta water, oranges, and a few tears. Today it will see paper.

I write three sentences on a notecard:

1. I will not pay for peace with parts of myself.
2. I will tell the truth the first time.
3. I will stop rehearsing my absence.

No poetry, just policy. I strike a wooden match, watch the first yellow bloom argue itself into steady orange, and touch flame to corner. The paper darkens, lifts, curls, and becomes what it always promised—ash that doesn't cling. I rinse the cooled remains down the drain. Not a ritual of rage. A ritual of release.

The apartment smells like smoke the way a story smells like a lesson after you finally listen. I open the window wider. Four in, four hold, six out. A siren far away blends into the hum under everything. I picture a bird with char on its feathers, eyes open.

> [Handwritten Affirmation: I choose clean heat over hidden smoke.]

I did not burn love. I burned the costumes. There's a difference. Costumes survive on applause; love survives on breath. I can keep loving the woman we finished without wearing the mask of the man I'm not.

On the table sits a small object I've ignored for weeks: a ceramic phoenix I bought in a museum gift shop years ago because I liked its stubborn posture. It faces left, tail arced, wings not yet open. I used to think it was about triumph—as if the point were to rise dramatically and make an entrance. Today it looks like engineering. Bone, tendon, torque. A design for carrying heat without being consumed by it.

I hold the figure in my palm. It's lighter than it looks. Maybe that's the lesson: the real thing weighs less than the performance of it.

Later, at the gym, I load the bar with what I can lift without theater. No grunting for strangers. No chasing a story about who I was at twenty-five. Five slow reps. Breath that counts. Knees like hinges that don't lie. I set the bar down gently each time and let the plates kiss the floor instead of attacking it. The body learns what you reward.

Back home I move the good chair under the window to catch the curve of afternoon light I keep missing by six inches. The plant approves. I sit. The room fits better. Small edits; big difference.

The phone vibrates with a text from a friend who knows how to ask cleanly: *How's your center?* I look down at my sternum like it can answer. I write back: *Quieter. Warmer. Not performing.* He sends back a fire emoji and a laughing face, because men are fluent in irony when intimacy feels too exposed. I send a single open palm. He gets it.

Grief visits like weather—arrives, lingers, moves on when it's done with its job. Today it rains once for five minutes while I stand in the doorway and let a few drops find my forearms. The water beads then slides off. The skin does what it was designed to do.

The kettle clicks. I pour, steep, wait. Patience tastes like plain tea. No honey. I sip and read the three lines I burned earlier, now copied into my notebook beside a small sketch of a rising bird. Next to it I draw a lotus—roots in what looks like a mess, petals unashamed of being clean. Fire and water. Both honest. Both needed.

> [Handwritten Affirmation: I rise by design, not by accident.]

When evening lays its coin of light on the ceiling again, I don't audition for it. I simply receive it. If a day is a kiln, this one fired me at the right temperature—hot enough to change shape, cool enough not to crack.

I place the ceramic phoenix on the bookshelf between the rice cooker manual and the thin book of poems I only like in winter. Not a shrine. A reminder. The room breathes.

Inhale four. Hold four. Exhale six. The heat is clean.

Ritual • Phoenix Practice (Day 3)

1. Write three lines you're ready to live without rehearsal. Keep them concrete (verbs over adjectives).
2. Burn safely over a sink or in a fire-safe dish; open a window. Watch until flame becomes ash.
3. Copy the three lines into your notebook. Draw a small phoenix or open palm beside them.
4. Stand with feet hip-width, knees soft. Inhale 4, hold 4, exhale 6 for 7 rounds.
5. Seal by taking ten deliberate steps through your home, placing one object in its right place.

Note: If flame isn't available or comfortable, tear the paper slowly into small pieces and soak them in water. The point is transformation, not drama.

Journal Prompts

- What did I burn today that was costume, not love?
- Where does clean heat live in my body—throat, chest, belly—and what sentence unlocks it?
- If my rising is engineering, what are the joints and bolts I need to check weekly?
- Name one performance I retire this month. What replaces it that's quieter and truer?
- Write three lines that begin: *I rise when I...*

Symbol Thread

- Phoenix (first reveal): not spectacle, structure—a design for carrying heat.
- Lotus: roots in honest mud, bloom without apology; pairs the phoenix's fire with water's steadiness.
- Open Palm: accompanies the burn—release without flinging, receive without clutching.

Chapter 4 - Compass & Arrow

Chapter 4 — Compass & Arrow

Epigraph
A clean yes makes a thousand noes unnecessary.

I stretch a strip of blue painter's tape across the floor from the door to the desk—my literal north. The line is not mystical; it's practical. I slide the chair so the back legs kiss a small X I penciled on the wood. I want the window in front of me, not behind. Light belongs on the face of things.

On a notecard I write: Today's aims—three only. Nothing heroic. Nothing that asks me to become a committee. I choose what makes the rest easier:

- Send the one message that removes a month of wondering.
- Move my body until my mind stops narrating.
- Put one object in its right place in every room.

Aim is mercy. Without it, I wander and call it work.

[Handwritten Affirmation: I aim before I move.]

The phone buzzes with an invitation that looks like old me—last-minute, loose, fueled by fear of missing something unnamed. I feel the clutch in my belly, then the breath—inhale 4, hold 4, exhale 6. My thumbs type without apology: *Not tonight. Protecting my aim. Have a good one.* I set the phone face down. The body registers the yes as relief, not loss.

The Phoenix/Lotus pairing sits on the shelf like a diagram I can read. Fire gives thrust. Water gives ballast. Direction needs both or you spend your heat spinning in place. I think of every time I mistook movement for aim—calendar full, heart empty. Today is different by inches, not miles, which is how real direction works.

I open the window a little wider and lift the plant to the sill. The air says grow and the plant listens. I would like to be that straightforward.

At the gym I keep the weights honest—no theater, no nostalgia. Five slow reps, three sets. The bar descends in a line I could draw with a ruler. Knees track over toes. Spine remembers it's a column, not a question mark. I leave with steadier legs and a cleaner head. Aim lives in angles, not slogans.

Back home, I re-read the first aim and send the message. No preamble, no hedge, just the truth I was willing to earn by breathing first. The delivery chime is small and decisive. Either way it answers, I have already chosen posture over performance.

The afternoon drifts toward gold. I place the ceramic phoenix so its beak points toward the window—toward light, not attention. Beside it, the lotus sketch I made last night—roots drawn as scribbles on purpose—leans in a frame. Heat and water; thrust and float. Under them I tape a thin strip that reads: Direction is what you repeat.

[Handwritten Affirmation: My yes chooses my orbit.]

By evening I notice the apartment has a path. The tape line on the floor is still there—door to desk—and a second one has appeared in my mind: sink to bed, bed to mat, mat to page. I walk it once on purpose, the way you test a trail after rain. It holds.

A friend calls and asks how I'm doing, which is different than asking what I'm doing. I tell him the truth—quieter, warmer, less pretending.

He says he's proud of me, then jokes about me becoming a monk. I laugh. I am not emptying my life; I am aiming it.

When the moon coins the ceiling again, I don't reposition myself to catch it. The light finds me where I already am. That feels like the whole point.

Ritual • North List (Day 4)

1. Draw a short line on paper—a tiny compass—then write N above it.
2. List three aims for today that, if done, make other choices simpler.
3. Set a twenty-five-minute timer. Pick the aim you'd avoid first.
4. Phone face down. Breath cadence 4–4–6 until the timer ends.
5. When done, take seven steps through your home and place one object right in each room. Call the route your path out loud.

Note: No adding aims midday. Protect the three. If one fails, the other two still count. Direction is repetition.

Journal Prompts

- What do I do that looks like movement but isn't aim?
- Which yes today made three noes unnecessary?
- Where in my body do I feel north, and what sentence supports it?
- What tiny corridor—door to desk, sink to bed—organizes my day without force?
- Write one paragraph that begins: *Direction is what I repeat...*

Symbol Thread

- Phoenix/Lotus continues—heat as thrust, water as ballast.
- Sagittarius arrow appears at the chapter's end—aim without strain.
- Compass rose watermark at the opener—orientation before acceleration.
- Open Palm margin icon beside the Ritual—release distraction, receive focus.

Chapter 5 - Lines and Doors

Chapter 5 — Lines & Doors

Epigraph
A good boundary isn't a wall. It's a door with hinges.

I make coffee and write four headings on a single page:

I offer.
I don't offer.
I request.
I release.

Under I offer I write: presence; clean heat; direct words; dates with a start and an end; leadership that listens.
Under I don't offer I write: secrecy; apologies for desire; performances; changing my center to keep a chair warm.
Under I request I write: honesty the first time; clear noes; check-ins after intensity; respect for my quiet hours.
Under I release I write: the need to be chosen by everyone; bargains with my breath; the version of me that kept the peace by leaving himself.

Four headings. One page. A door with hinges.

Before I send anything to anyone, I do the math of breath—inhale 4, hold 4, exhale 6—until my thumbs will type without pleading. A message waits on my phone from someone who deserves exactness, not theater.

> *Hey—you're luminous and I enjoy us. My life is aimed right now.*
> *I move with intention and I don't do exclusivity. I'm honest,*
> *warm, and steady. If ease and clarity fit you, let's keep exploring.*
> *If not, thank you for the light we shared.*

I read it out loud once to hear if any word tries to hide. Then I add one more line because languages are bridges:

> *Quiero movernos con intención, con claridad y respeto. Si no es para ti, está bien. Gracias por tu energía.*

Send.

The body registers the boundary as relief. Not loss. Relief. I set the phone face down and rinse the cup.

[Handwritten Affirmation: My kindness has edges.]

Later, we meet. A bar that plays music quiet enough to hear each other. I choose a chair that lets me face the door; not paranoia—design. She arrives in denim and directness. We laugh before we order. It's simple to enjoy someone when you are not auditioning.

We talk about lives that now have corridors in them—hers, mine. The conversation finds a shape, the almond overlap where two circles meet. *Vesica piscis.* Two truths, one shared space. I name what I can hold. She names what she won't.

— *Her:* "So... you're seeing others."
— *Me:* "Yes. With integrity. With clarity. Quietly."
— *Her:* "And you'll tell me if that changes."
— *Me:* "I will. And I'll listen if your needs change."
— *Her:* "I want softness, but not guessing."
— *Me:* "We can do softness. We don't do guessing."

We do not pretend this is a negotiation to win. It's an architecture check. Load-bearing tests. How much truth can the frame carry without cracking? Enough, it turns out, when the joints are honest.

The server brings a second round and we settle into the kind of silence that doesn't panic. My hand rests open on the table. She places two fingers in the center of my palm. An answer without a paragraph.

> [Handwritten Affirmation: I state terms with an open palm.]

After, we walk. City air. The moon lays its white coin on a parked car's hood. She asks one more clean question:

— *Her:* "If I call you at midnight?"
— *Me:* "I won't answer. I protect my north. But I'll return it in the morning."
— *Her:* "Good. I like men who sleep."

We smile. The door with hinges swings both ways.

Back home, I set the ceramic Phoenix to face the window and slide the Lotus sketch closer. Fire for thrust. Water for ballast. Direction for both. In the middle, the overlap—the place where two whole lives meet without erasing edges. I tape today's four-heading page to the inside of a cabinet I open every morning. Teeth. Coffee. Terms.

Sleep comes easy when you stop using your yes to lie.

Ritual • The Open-Palm Script (Day 5)

1. On one page, write the four headings: I offer / I don't offer / I request / I release.
2. Under each, list three concrete items (verbs and nouns, not adjectives).

3. Read the page out loud once. Cross any word that begs. Replace it with a verb.
4. Choose one person who deserves clarity. Send a message you could read to a friend without cringing.
5. After sending, stand with feet hip-width. Breath cadence 4–4–6 for seven rounds. Whisper: *Exact is kind.*

Note: If you don't have someone to message, send it to yourself. Integrity rehearses.

Boundary Language (examples you can steal)

- *"I like our pace. I won't do late-night texting. I'm free most mornings after nine."*
- *"I'm not exclusive. If that doesn't fit, thank you for telling me now."*
- *"I desire you. I also protect my alone time. Both are true."*
- *"I won't keep secrets for chemistry."*
- *"If we feel heat, let's plan it rather than drift."*
- *"A clean no is welcome. Please use it."*
- *"If I go quiet, I'm recalibrating, not punishing. I'll say when I'm back."*
- *"I won't be managed. I will be clear."*

Journal Prompts

- Where did I over-explain a no? What would the exact sentence be next time?
- What do I genuinely offer in relationship that costs me little but means a lot?
- Which request feels brave to write and simple to honor?

- Draw two circles for me and the other. What belongs only in mine? Only in theirs? What belongs in the overlap?
- Finish: *My kindness has edges when...* and *I keep the door hinged by...*

Symbol Thread

- Phoenix/Lotus continues—heat with ballast; attraction with dignity.
- Vesica Piscis foregrounded as the overlap of two whole lives; not merger, meeting.
- Open Palm as the boundary icon—release without flinging; receive without clutching.
- Sagittarius arrow returns as a small end-mark—aimed connection, not scattered sparks.

Chapter 6 - Gravity & Grace

Chapter 6 — Gravity & Grace

Epigraph
Discipline is the floor; tenderness is the air.

The metronome app clicks softly on the counter—sixty beats, steady as a heart that isn't auditioning. I set two mugs down beside a small card I titled last night: Cadence. Four lines, clean ink.

Check-in.
Connection.
Recovery.
Departure.

Not romance by spreadsheet—posture by design. Gravity keeps the room from floating apart; grace keeps us from bracing.

I text her:
Tonight, seven to ten. Phones down after the first ten minutes. A check-in tomorrow at ten a.m.—ten minutes, voice only. If either of us turns yellow, we say so.
She replies with a feather emoji and a thumbs-up. Feather for grace. Thumb for yes.

> [Handwritten Affirmation: I schedule warmth without strangling it.]

I block the time on my calendar. The square of color looks small and honest. A day can carry more love than noise when you give it a spine.

Afternoon light lands on the ceramic Phoenix and the framed Lotus sketch—heat and ballast—even now pointing at the window like a quiet compass. I add a thin spiral I drew on scrap paper and tape it beneath them. Not a vortex; a staircase. Around and up, each loop a level you earn.

Four in, four hold, six out. The body remembers the floor.

Evening comes in a soft hurry. We meet at my place. Shoes by the door. Hands washed. We stand in the kitchen and do the short version of what used to take an evening:

— *Capacity?*
— *Green with a streak of yellow—long week.*
— *Noted. Mine's green. We can keep the pace tender.*

The check-in is three minutes. No essays. Facts, then breath. We set the timer for thirty. We move the good chair by the window; we sit close enough to hear the other breathe. Gravity: the timer, the corridor of three hours, the promise of a clean end. Grace: the way we let silence talk first.

At nine fifty-five, the timer taps the counter like a polite guest. We stand. We do the departure we agreed to:

1. Name one thing you received.
2. Name one boundary you honored.
3. Name one sentence to carry.

— *Her:* "I received steadiness. I honored leaving my phone face down. I'll carry 'exact is kind.'"
— *Me:* "I received your attention. I honored my north. I'll carry 'softness without guessing.'"

No after-midnight drift. The door with hinges swings without squeak. We bless the room with a look. She pulls on her denim jacket. We hug like people who know when to stop. I text after she leaves: *Thank you for tonight's cadence.* She replies: *Gracias por tu estructura y tu suavidad.* Structure and softness. Gravity and grace in two languages.

[Handwritten Affirmation: Cadence protects desire.]

Later, alone, I rinse the two mugs and listen to the apartment's small sounds—the refrigerator hum, the pipe's warm tick, a car easing into a parallel park outside. The world keeps its beat. I slide the Cadence card into the cabinet with the toothbrush so I'll see it in the morning. Discipline is easier when it lives where your hands already go.

Not every night will land this clean. That's what grace is for—the recovery arc when life talks back.

I sketch it on the spiral:

- Green — proceed with tenderness.
- Yellow — slow the pace, lower the volume, shorten the window.
- Red — stop and name it; reschedule after a pause and a walk.

Recovery is not punishment; it's maintenance. I set a reminder for tomorrow's ten-minute voice call. Cadence turns moments into a life.

When the moon lays its coin on the ceiling, I stay where I already am. Floor under me, air around me. The body says yes.

Ritual • The Cadence Check-In (Day 6)

1. Draw a small spiral on paper. Title it Cadence.

2. With your person (or solo), agree to a three-minute pre-connection check-in: Capacity (Green/Yellow/Red) • Desire (one sentence) • Boundary (one sentence).
3. Set a clear window (e.g., seven to ten). Use a timer for the first thirty to settle phones, pace, and breath.
4. Close with a Departure Three: *received* • *boundary honored* • *sentence to carry.*
5. Schedule a ten-minute voice debrief the next day. Keep it exact.
6. Breath cadence 4–4–6 bookends both calls. Whisper: *Cadence protects desire.*

Remote option: If apart, do the same by voice. Cameras optional. Voice tells the truth with fewer costumes.

Micro-Scripts (use, adapt, translate)

- *"Capacity check: I'm yellow—low sleep. I want closeness, low volume. No analysis tonight."*
- *"Boundary: I'll leave by ten. I'll text when home. No midnight loops."*
- *"Recovery: I turned red. Let's reschedule after I sleep. Thank you for choosing the floor with me."*
- *"Desire: I want warmth and quiet presence. Let's let silence lead for the first ten."*
- *"Departure: I received your attention. I honored my north."*

Journal Prompts

- Where does my life speed up when I'm afraid, and how does cadence slow me without shutting me down?

- What three structures (sleep, food, calendar) act as gravity for me?
- Where can I offer grace without rescuing or performing?
- Write a recovery script you won't be ashamed to send at two in the afternoon.
- Finish: *Desire lasts when...* and *We keep the hinges oiled by...*

Symbol Thread

- Phoenix/Lotus remains at the altar—thrust + float as the background of cadence.
- Spiral appears for iterative practice—a staircase, not a whirlpool.
- Feather marks grace notes in the margins.
- Open Palm accompanies the Departure Three—receive, release, carry.

Chapter 7 -Edges & Embers

Chapter 7 — Edges & Embers

Epigraph
Heat that lasts knows where not to burn.

The skillet holds yesterday's warmth the way a good promise does—low, steady, ready. I turn the flame to the smallest blue that will keep it honest. No smoke. No show. Just enough.

On a card by the stove I write two words: Edges and Embers.

Edges—the lines that keep the field from turning to ash.
Embers—the small, bright signals we feed so the fire doesn't beg for drama.

> [Handwritten Affirmation: I keep the heat without burning the field.]

I send a text that is both invitation and architecture:

This week: two embers, one kindling, one fire.
— Embers: 5–10 min voice, phones down after.
— Kindling: a walk or tea, one hour.
— Fire: a three-hour window, cadence rules.
Green/Yellow/Red applies. Let's name edges tonight.

She replies with a flame, a leaf, and a droplet. Fire, ballast, grace. Phoenix / Lotus / Spiral in emojis. We're getting fluent.

The day moves like a clean river. At six, she arrives with quiet shoulders. We sit at the table with two pens and one small bowl of olives because a little salt makes honesty easier.

I draw three columns and title them Green, Yellow, Red. Edges, not edicts. Living lines.

Green (welcome without effort): truth the first time; phones face down; arrivals and departures on time; check-ins by voice; walking side-by-side without filling the air.
Yellow (curious, go slow): more frequency; late starts; weekends away later; meeting each other's circles with care.
Red (no): secrets; triangulating; midnight fights; anything that asks us to lie to our breath.

We read them out loud. Not a negotiation—an orientation. The field gets its fence; the spark gets its space.

> [Handwritten Affirmation: I choose edges that deepen presence, not drama.]

We add a Signal Lexicon because bodies speak quicker than paragraphs:

- One tap on the wrist: slow the pace.
- Two taps: pause; breath check.
- Open palm shown: capacity check (say your color).
- Small nod with eye contact: "I'm here, I'm with you."
- Hand to chest once: "I need a minute—stay close."

No codes for secrecy; only cues for care. The point isn't clever. The point is clean.

We test it the same night. Mid-conversation I feel my mind start to sprint—the old reflex to outrun tenderness with talk. She gives one tap. I breathe 4–4–6 without announcing it. The sprint dissolves. We're back.

We close with the Departure Three we learned—received, boundary honored, sentence to carry—and she leaves at the time we set. The room stays warm, not haunted. The skillet, rinsed, still holds a whisper of heat.

The week unrolls.

Ember #1 (Tuesday): a five-minute voice note after her shift—no fixing, just witness. "Green with a yellow stripe," she says. I reply with silence first, then one sentence: "I hear your grit." Embers are not about quantity; they're about signal fidelity.

Kindling (Thursday): tea, one hour. A walk to the corner where the streetlight throws a soft coin on the sidewalk. We stop there like it's a ritual site. We practice two taps in the wild when the city gets loud. The taps become a tiny bridge.

Ember #2 (Saturday): a note before bed: *Gracias por tu suavidad y tu estructura.* I screenshot it because some sentences are fuel later.

Fire (Sunday): three hours by the window, phones in a drawer, timer set. Laughter. Quiet. The Phoenix figure faces the light; the Lotus sketch leans like a shoulder. We don't sprint. We simmer. Drama is easy heat; presence is harder and better.

I start a page in the notebook called Ember Log. Not a diary—an inventory of glow:

- "Two fingers in my palm—answer without paragraph."
- "Her laugh when the kettle clicked."
- "We left on time. Felt powerful."
- "Signal worked—two taps saved the night."

Direction is repetition. Cadence turns moments into a life.

By the second week, the field feels more alive, not restricted. This is the part nobody tells you: firebreaks make more room for flame. When we draw a clean line and keep it, we can actually see the fire. When we don't, all we see is smoke.

At the gym, I load a weight I can control even when tired. The bar kisses the floor each rep. I think about the edge of form—where strength ends and strain begins. I stop on the rep before ego would make a mess. The body nods. It remembers that week after week is a louder signal than any single max. Embers over spectacle.

That night I tape a thin strip under the Phoenix/Lotus pair: Edges keep heat honest. Embers keep heat here. The room seems to breathe with me.

[Handwritten Affirmation: Small signals, steady flame.]

I fall asleep listing five bright specks from the day. Not gratitude as performance; gratitude as oxygen. The moon lays its coin on the ceiling. I leave it where it lands.

Ritual • The Ember Map (Week Rhythm)

1. Name your edges: make a three-column list—Green / Yellow / Red—for this season of your life. Keep it revisable.
2. Set the cadence: schedule two embers (5–10 min), one kindling (≤1 hr), one fire (≤3 hrs) this week. Protect starts and ends.
3. Build your Signal Lexicon with your person (or for friendships/family): choose 3–5 cues from the list (or invent your own). Practice once in a calm moment.

4. Make an Ember Log: one page where you jot five bright moments per week (one line each).
5. Review & adjust on Sunday: move one Yellow to Green or Red; refine one signal; choose your next week's windows.
6. Bookend each connection with breath 4–4–6. Whisper: *Small signals, steady flame.*

Solo version: Use the same cadence with yourself: two embers (brief creative moments), one kindling (an hour for body or art), one fire (a three-hour deep work or deep rest block).

Micro-Scripts (edge talk without theater)

- *"Green: walks, voice notes, face-down phones, on-time exits. Yellow: more frequency—ask first. Red: secrecy."*
- *"If I tap twice, let's pause and breathe. If you need a minute, hand to chest once—no disappearing."*
- *"I'd like two embers this week—a five-minute call and a voice note. Sunday three-hour window works?"*
- *"I stop where strain begins. That's where desire stays warm."*
- *"Necesito bajar el volumen, no la verdad."* (I need to lower the volume, not the truth.)

Journal Prompts

- Where did I confuse smoke for heat? What would be an ember instead?
- Which edge today protected me from performing?

- What are my top three Green edges right now? One Yellow I'm curious about? One Red I needed to say out loud?
- What five bright specks can I log from this week without adjectives?
- Finish: *Firebreaks make more room for flame when...*

Symbol Thread

- Phoenix/Lotus continue: thrust + float as the background of sustained heat.
- Ember (new icon): a small coal with a quiet glow—used beside the Ember Log callouts.
- Open Palm marks the Signal Lexicon margin notes.
- Spiral returns to signify iteration—edges and embers refined weekly.
- Vesica Piscis appears as the overlap where shared edges live.

Chapter 8 - Fields & Firebreaks

Chapter 8 — Fields & Firebreaks

Epigraph
More people doesn't mean more fire. It means cleaner lines.

The circles are drawn, the map taped to the inside of a kitchen cabinet where I reach for mugs. I like that: boundaries where my hands already go. Every morning the rings look back at me with the same question— *Who gets what, when, and how?* It's not about worth. It's about access.

I test the map three times in one day.

Family. My mother wants to talk before work. She calls at seven-thirty with a voice that sounds like cinnamon toast and caution. The old me would answer anywhere, anyhow. The mapped me texts first: *8:15 voice? I'm on breath and coffee till then.* She replies with a heart. At 8:15 we talk about the little things that are the big thing. I hang up and feel the field freshly watered, not trampled.

Work. A calendar invite arrives without an agenda. I decline with a note: *"Happy to join—can you add the decision we're making?"* Ten minutes later the update lands. Decision added. Length cut to twenty minutes. The meeting earns its keep and the day keeps its spine.

Public. In my comments a stranger writes like a siren: *"Urgent—DM me now."* I breathe 4–4–6 until the urge to perform fades, then answer with the line I promised myself: *"Thanks for being here. I respond during office hours; DMs aren't for coaching. Here's the inquiry link."* The comment sits there like a small fence and a welcome mat at once.

[Handwritten Affirmation: Public isn't permission.]

At dinner with cousins, a story grows teeth. I feel the table tilt toward spectacle. I place my palm face-up between the glasses—Open Palm—and say, *"I'll pass on that version. I want to keep us kind."* The room exhales. Someone asks about my book instead and the conversation moves from trial to craft. Firebreak installed; laughter returns.

Back home, I revise the rings like a gardener. One friend shifts from Inner to Middle for a season—not a punishment, a pause. Another moves from Middle to Inner after showing up three Thursdays in a row with tea and their phone already face down. The map breathes. I add dates in pencil.

I draft a Public Note that will one day live on a website, but tonight it lives in my notebook:

I reply within 48–72 hours. I don't coach by DM. I keep my mornings for breath, writing, and quiet. If I miss you, it's because I'm protecting the work that made you want to reach out. Thank you for meeting me at the door, not the window.

[Handwritten Affirmation: I'm generous within form.]

The week ends with a backyard birthday—folding chairs, citronella, neighbors who say your name like a question and a blessing. A man I barely know tries to pull me into a late-night debate that smells like gasoline. I smile and use the Sagittarius in me: *"I'm off duty tonight. Walk me to the cooler and tell me what you're making lately."* He talks about a tomato vine that refuses to quit. We trade recipes. The field stays green.

Before sleep I look at the Phoenix and Lotus, the old lesson made practical: thrust and float. Expansion without erosion. The moon lays its coin on the ceiling and I let it be the moon again—no job to do, just light.

[Handwritten Affirmation: I expand with edges, not excuses.]

Ritual • Field Survey (30 minutes) *(kept — see worksheet)*

(You've got the PDF. Use pencil. Review monthly. Breathe 4–4–6.)

Journal Prompts

- Who moved rings this month and why?
- Which five Firebreaks saved the field this week?
- Write your three-sentence Public Note and cut one sentence.
- Where did access without cadence drain you? What cadence repairs it?
- Finish: *I am generous within form when...*

Symbol Thread

- Vesica Piscis at shared edges; Open Palm for scripts; Spiral on monthly reviews; Ember beside small weekly wins.

Chapter 9 - Crowd & Center

Chapter 9 — Crowd & Center

Epigraph
The room can have you without taking you.

The flyer says seven p.m., doors at six-thirty. I arrive at six with a satchel that holds less than my nerves: water, notecards, a small towel, a pen, a mint. In the mirror of the venue bathroom I look more rested than I feel. I press one hand to my sternum, one to my belly. Breath 4–4–6 until the spin becomes a lane.

I tape a tiny strip of blue painter's tape on the inside of my wrist—the same tape I use to mark the floor from door to desk. When I catch it later under stage light, it will remind me of my north.

Backstage, the green room is beige and humming. A volunteer asks if I need anything. "A chair near the door and five minutes of quiet," I say. They nod and the room re-arranges. Gravity established.

I set a timer for three minutes and read a card titled Center Routine:

- Capacity: Green with a yellow stripe.
- Aim: One sentence: *Tell the truth the first time.*
- Boundary: One sentence: *No stories I haven't metabolized.*
- Gesture: Open palm once to remember the room is an invitation, not a verdict.

I roll my shoulders. Knees soft. Spine remembers it's a column. The Phoenix on my shelf is not here, but the architecture is.

> [Handwritten Affirmation: I share from a center I get to keep.]

On stage, the light is patient. The faces are coins at first, then eyes. I start with breath the audience can hear: "Inhale four, hold four, release six." Some bodies obey, some smile, some resist. All fine. I tell them why I'm here: *to practice a life that stays warm without burning the house.* The line lands like a chair set down without noise.

I give them stories I've already lived enough to own. When I reach for a line that still stings, I put a hand to my chest and move on. No unprocessed pain on display. The room can have honesty without getting the first draft of my wounds.

A phone flashes. I don't scold; I slow: "If you're grabbing this, take the line, not the man." Laughter. The line they take is the one I can stand behind tomorrow.

The Q&A begins. A woman asks for advice I won't give in public. I use the Open Palm: "That's a tender question. Try this tonight—capacity, desire, boundary—and keep the results for yourself. I don't do diagnosis from a stage." She nods. The room nods with her.

A man in the second row performs urgency. "But what about when people won't respect your no?" I breathe my answer before I speak it. "Then your exit is your edge. Boundaries without exits are wishes." He leans back. The room exhales.

When it ends, applause feels like a tide I can surf without drowning. I thank them and walk to the signing table without stealing one more minute to soak in what doesn't belong to me. Leaving on time keeps heat honest.

The line is a river of hands and names. I keep my Signal Lexicon alive with strangers—one tap on the table when I need to slow, small nod when I'm here, two taps for a breath. The line moves like mercy.

Interlude — Two Fingers in an Open Palm

She didn't grab. She placed. Two fingers like a bridge laid gently across the smallest river. Not claim, not clutch—answer. Her eyes didn't audition; they steadied. The gesture read me as if she'd studied the same lexicon: *one open palm = I'm here, present, unhurried.* There was play in it, yes, but also literacy. That's what pulled at me—the rare mix of signal and restraint.

For a moment the room blurred and the almond shape appeared—the *vesica piscis* where public overlaps the personal without erasing either. In that lens I saw possibility, not extraction; warmth, not spectacle.

[Handwritten Affirmation: Heat without hurry.]

Similarities (the overlap):

- We both speak in small signals rather than speeches.
- A shared preference for quiet presence over display.
- Heat with good posture—eye contact that doesn't take.

Differences (the edges):

- Her invitation arrived as immediacy; mine lives in cadence.
- Her fire tilted toward spark; mine toward steady flame.
- She seemed to trust the moment; I trust the window I've already chosen.

Why I didn't fully engage: because my center routine forbids first-draft choices under bright light; because the map matters—this was Outer/Middle ring territory, not Core; because my capacity was green with a yellow stripe and I had promised myself no new stories on stage; because leaving on time keeps heat honest. Most of all, because I want a life where desire is answered by design. Clean heat or no heat.

If alignment is real—tonight or ten years from now—it won't require a chase. It will look like two practiced fires meeting at the edge of a well-kept field: an ember first (a voice note, five minutes), kindling next (an hour, phones down), then fire by agreement (a window with a door and a clock). Phoenix for thrust. Lotus for ballast. The overlap stays clear. And what is will reveal itself without being dragged into being.

[Handwritten Affirmation: I prefer ignition by design.]

I sign the next book, write her name carefully, and keep the door hinged. The crowd is still a crowd; my center is still mine.

I walk to my car with one bag and less noise. The blue tape on my wrist is a little frayed. Good. It did its job.

At home, I rinse the empty water bottle and write a Crowd Debrief in the notebook:

- Received: the quiet when the room breathed together.
- Boundary honored: no new stories told on stage.
- Sentence to carry: *The room can have you without taking you.*

[Handwritten Affirmation: I exit clean.]

I put the pen down. The apartment hums. The moon coins the ceiling again and I don't perform for it. Center, kept.

Ritual • Greenroom Cadence (Pre/Post)

Before (6 minutes)

1. Breath 4–4–6 (2 minutes).
2. Write one-line Capacity / Aim / Boundary (1 minute).
3. Speak your thesis aloud once (1 minute).

4. Mark your north (tape on wrist / talisman in pocket) (30 sec).
5. Phone face down; place visible clock (30 sec).
6. Gesture: Open palm once; small nod to yourself (1 minute).

After (5 minutes)

1. Departure Three: *received / boundary honored / sentence to carry.*
2. Exit on time (no bonus minutes).
3. Hydrate and text one Inner person.
4. Don't read DMs until morning.
5. Replace tape/talisman where it lives; breathe once more.

Micro-Scripts (stage • afterparty • online)

- *"I don't do first-draft feelings on stage."*
- *"That question deserves quiet. Try Cadence tonight and keep the results."*
- *"Thank you for the invite—I leave by ten."*
- *"I don't coach by DM. Office hours are on my site."*
- *"I'm here to share what I've metabolized, not to perform pain."*
- *"Let's keep this in the Middle ring—no personal histories."*
- *Spanish: "Esa pregunta es delicada. Prefiero que la trabajes en privado con la práctica de Cadencia."*

Journal Prompts

- What did the crowd give me that I can keep without borrowing identity?

- Where did I bend toward performance? What signal brought me back?
- Which part of my Center Routine saved me tonight?
- Draft a two-sentence Public Q&A policy I can say with a smile.
- Finish: *Leaving on time keeps heat honest when...*

Symbol Thread

- Compass/Arrow for north on the wrist; Open Palm at the mic; Vesica at the signing table; Phoenix/Lotus as backstage altar; Spiral in repetition of events.

Chapter 10 - Harvest & Habit

Chapter 10 — Harvest & Habit

Epigraph
Yield belongs to rhythm.

Morning is ordinary on purpose. The metronome breathes its soft sixty. I rinse a mug, open the cabinet, and the Field Survey page looks back at me. Boundaries where my hands already go. Today I'm after the quiet math of a season—the proof that repetition becomes fruit.

On a card I write five words and pin it to the fridge with a small magnet:

Seed. Sow. Tend. Harvest. Rest.

[Handwritten Affirmation: I reap what I repeat.]

I choose floors, not ceilings. Floors I can stand on every day without theater. Three habits, season-length:

- Breath bookends (4–4–6 on wake and before sleep).
- Movement honest (five sets I can control, not perform).
- North in sight (painter's tape on the wrist or the floor).

That's it. Outcome is a rumor; habits are the plan.

I take a Harvest Walk through my apartment, touching the things that have learned to help me: the chair that catches morning light, the plant that tells the truth about water, the taped line door→desk, the Phoenix/Lotus pair that faces the window like quiet teachers. I say aloud, *"Direction is repetition."* The room agrees.

At the desk I draw a small Season Wheel—thirteen empty wedges for thirteen weeks. I title the wheel Loom because this is how a life is woven: the same threads passing through at a rhythm the hands can keep. I write my three habits in the margin and a single sentence of *why* for each. Reasons keep form when mood forgets.

[Handwritten Affirmation: Consistency is kindness to my future.]

I don't track with punishment; I track with witness. Checks, not scolding. Ink, not shame. On the back of the card I list Honest Metrics—measures that tell me whether the field is alive:

- Sleep met (yes/no)
- Breath bookends (yes/no)
- Moved without theater (yes/no)
- Exits on time (yes/no)
- Ember Log entries (0–5 lines/week)
- Green/Yellow/Red named (yes/no)

No calorie algebra. No virtue spreadsheet. Just whether I kept my deals with myself.

Each evening I do a Small Harvest—five bright specks from the day, one line each, no adjectives. Evidence. Some days the specks are soft crumbs—kettle click, tape line, two mugs rinsed. Some days they're warm slices—clear no, honest yes. All days, the same question: *What did I strengthen by repeating it?*

If I miss a habit, I don't perform regret. I compost it. Compost is where yesterday's undones become tomorrow's soil: a six-minute walk after dinner instead of a long penance; a glass of water and lights out at ten when I wanted drama. I'm not interested in being right; I'm interested in being ready.

[Handwritten Affirmation: Recovery is maintenance, not a trial.]

Every seventh week I go fallow—a deliberate under-schedule to keep the loom from snapping. Less load, same floors. Breath, movement, north. More light on the page, more walking, longer exits. Fallow isn't quitting; it's keeping what you grew.

At the gym I stop one rep before ego would make a mess. The bar kisses the floor each time. The body understands habit better than speeches. On the walk home I pass two people arguing and feel the old tilt toward spectacle. I practice a tiny harvest in real time: silence, breath, pace that keeps my nervous system mine. Some yields don't look like fruit; they look like a life I can stand inside.

Las cosechas siguen al ritmo. Harvest follows rhythm. I like how that sounds in Spanish—round and inevitable.

At night, the moon coins the ceiling. I don't audition for it. I whisper the season sentence I chose for this quarter: *Repeat what returns you.* The room breathes.

[Handwritten Affirmation: Repeat what returns you.]

Ritual • Season Loom (13-Week Cycle)

1. Draw a circle and divide into 13 wedges. Title it Loom.
2. Choose 3 floor-habits (daily). Keep them embarrassingly doable.

3. For each, write one sentence why. Tape the Loom where your hands already go.
4. Define Honest Metrics (4–6 yes/no signals) on the back.
5. Mark each day with a simple check. No red X's. Misses get composted (write a one-line pivot).
6. Week 7 = Fallow: protect floors, lighten loads, extend exits.
7. Week 13 = Harvest Week: tally checks, read the Ember Log, choose one habit to upgrade by one inch.
8. Breath 4–4–6 at wake and sleep all season.

Solo/Partnered option: Share Looms during a ten-minute voice on Sundays. Witness, don't fix.

Micro-Scripts (to defend the loom)

- *"I keep Sundays fallow this season. I can do Thursday at 6."*
- *"I'm on a 13-week loom. Floors only, not projects."*
- *"I leave by nine; leaving on time keeps my season."*
- *"I'm choosing steady flame over spark tonight."*
- *Spanish: "Estoy en temporada de ritmo; mantengo lo esencial."*

Journal Prompts

- What did I repeat this week that returned me?
- Which habit is a floor pretending to be a ceiling—shrink it one inch.
- Where did compost turn a miss into soil?
- List five bright specks from the day without adjectives. What pattern do they point to?

- Finish: *Fallow protects my yield when...*

Honest Metrics (examples to copy)

- Sleep $\geq$ 7h (yes/no)
- Breath bookends (yes/no)
- Movement honest (yes/no)
- Exits on time (yes/no)
- 1 Ember Log entry/day (yes/no)
- Green/Yellow/Red named (yes/no)

(Pick six. Retire one each season; add one new.)

Symbol Thread

- Spiral marks the Loom—same path, higher level.
- Ember beside daily checks—small glow > spectacle.
- Phoenix/Lotus anchors the page—thrust + float baked into routine.
- Open Palm icon near Compost—release shame, keep learning.
- Vesica Piscis at Harvest Week—overlap of practice and proof.

Chapter 11 - Reflections Reflected

Chapter 11 — Reflections Reflected

(Keeping the Endless Becoming Practice)

Epigraph
We should not ignore what we see and sense and feel.

Morning gives me three mirrors before I find glass: the kettle's belly, the window, the quiet in my chest. I meet all three. I don't add makeup made of meaning. I let each reflect, then I practice the part that matters—what I do with what I notice.

On the counter a card reads:

See. Sense. Say. Stay.

See what is here.
Sense where it lands in the body.
Say one exact sentence.
Stay long enough for the next clean action.

> [Handwritten Affirmation: I witness without erasing.]

See. The plant's soil is dry; a new boundary felt easy last night; I flinched when a friend went quiet.
Sense. Throat open, belly calm, a prickle behind the sternum.
Say. *The soil needs water. Exactness fit me. I was afraid I'd be asked to perform.*
Stay. Fill the watering can. Keep the boundary. Text: *"I noticed myself tense when we went quiet. Nothing to fix; just naming."*

Reflection is not rumination. Rumination loops. Reflection lands. Rumination auditions; reflection accepts.

I stand before the hallway mirror and look at the face I keep finding. Some days I am tempted to edit—angles, shadows, history. Today I agree with the evidence. The man looking back is not a project; he is a participant. When I lift an Open Palm to the glass, he returns it. That's enough theology for a Tuesday.

> [Handwritten Affirmation: I accept the data and then choose the dance.]

The Vesica Piscis appears in the day's overlap—what I perceive and what I practice. Sight meets structure, sensation meets schedule. No erasure, just the almond lens that lets two truths coexist: *I am still becoming* and *I have already become.*

At the desk I copy a small line above today's tasks: Becoming is a spiral, not a ladder. Ladders argue worth at every rung. Spirals return, higher, kinder. I have circled this ground before—breath, boundary, presence— and each loop has made the floor stronger.

I walk the apartment the way I walk a field I'm responsible for— checking firebreaks, touching the taped line door→desk, letting the Phoenix/Lotus duo remind me that heat with ballast is the only fire I trust. The room is a mirror too. It reflects the shape of my habits back to me without insult.

I think of the woman who placed two fingers in my open palm, of family who test the edge and soften, of rooms that breathe in chorus. Reflection keeps attraction from turning into spectacle, keeps history from hardening into performance. Seeing clearly is not cold. It's merciful.

[Handwritten Affirmation: I keep becoming on purpose.]

When night lays its coin on the ceiling, I practice one more mirror—the one inside my ribs. Breath 4–4–6. Inventory without trial:

- What I saw: impatience around noon, tenderness at five.
- What I sensed: jaw loosened after the walk.
- What I said: one clean no.
- How I stayed: I ended on time.

I do not give myself a verdict. I give myself continuity.

Ritual • Mirror Ledger (5 minutes, a.m. + p.m.)

Morning (2 minutes)

1. See: name 3 visible facts (no adjectives).
2. Sense: point to 1 body location and name the sensation (word or image).
3. Say: write 1 exact sentence (present tense, no apology).
4. Stay: schedule 1 small action aligned to the sentence.

Night (3 minutes)

1. Read the morning sentence aloud.
2. Log 4 S's: *What I Saw / Sensed / Said / how I Stayed.*
3. Whisper: *I witness without erasing.* Breath 4–4–6 × 3.

Note: If the mind starts narrating, return to facts and felt sense. Spiral, don't spiral out.

Micro-Scripts (reflection without rumination)

- *"Fact: my chest tightened; sentence: I need five quiet minutes."*
- *"I saw myself rush. I'm choosing a slower exit."*
- *"I sense heat. I'll put it in practice, not a performance."*
- *"Lo noté en mi cuerpo; voy a honrarlo sin drama."*

Journal Prompts

- What am I seeing that I've been editing? Name it without adjectives.
- Where does my body signal yes and how can I practice it tomorrow?
- Write one sentence you're willing to say out loud this week.
- How did I stay with myself when an old script invited performance?
- Finish: *Becoming is endless and kind when...*

Symbol Thread

- Vesica Piscis as the lens between perception and practice.
- Open Palm beside the Mirror Ledger—receive, then act.
- Spiral for the returns that rise.
- Phoenix/Lotus quietly in the margin—heat + ballast inside acceptance.
- First-Quarter Moon divider—becoming mid-cycle, not yet full, already more.

Chapter 12 - Returns, Reverence & Your Landing

Chapter 12 — Returns, Reverence & Your Landing

(A Private "Final" Chapter for the Reader) (longest, by design)

Epigraph
Choose where you will stand; let the standing choose you back.

Morning is ordinary on purpose. Breath 4–4–6. A hand to chest, a hand to belly. The quiet coin of moon is gone, and day puts a soft palm on your shoulder. This chapter is not about my shore. It is about yours.

This is your private "final"—the page you write on, the vow you keep, the terrain you name. It gathers what we practiced—discipline & desire, cadence & boundary, phoenix & lotus, open palm, vesica piscis, spiral— and hands them to you like tools in a small, well-oiled kit. You will choose your geography. You will draft your vows. You will set your cadence. You will write your poem. You will walk away with a map that fits in a pocket and expands like a horizon.

> [Handwritten Affirmation: What returns deserves a bow; what begins deserves a breath.]

---

0) The Cartographer's Table (Set the room)

Place these nearby: a pen; one small bowl of water; a coin or stone; a timer; any photo or object that names the life you want (optional). Put your phone face down. Breath 4–4–6 for 7 rounds. Whisper: *Exact is kind.*

I. Choose Your Terrain (Name your now)

Pick the landscape that sparks in your ribs. You may circle more than one. You may rename them. You may change later. Dignity lives where truth and timing overlap.

Island — You keep edges clear and invite with a dock. Freedom with form.
Peninsula — Mostly yours, sometimes shared; you practice seasonal closeness.
Continent — Abundance and lanes; you need structure to avoid scatter.
Mountain Top — Clarity, thin air; you schedule descents for warmth and food.
Mountain Base — Grounded, patient; you climb in windows, not on impulse.
River — Moving truth; you need banks (edges) so current doesn't flood.
Forest — Depth and shade; you mark paths so mystery nourishes, not hides.
Desert — Wide silence; you keep a water plan and a night-sky ritual.
City — Many doors; you set office hours and a north line you can see.
Inland Landmass — Stable, fertile; you guard against ruts by seeding surprise.
Water (Open Sea) — Vast; you chart by stars—cadence or you drift.

Write the name of your terrain: _____

One sentence why (present tense):
"I stand here because..." _____

[Handwritten Affirmation: I land without apology.]

II. Vows by Terrain (Freedom with form)

Choose 3–7 vows. Keep them short, speakable, repeatable. Steal, adapt, or write your own.

All Terrains (core vows)

- I keep breath bookends (4–4–6 on waking and sleep).
- I honor edges (Green/Yellow/Red) and exits on time.
- I choose ember → kindling → fire (no spectacle heat).
- I use my open palm for clarity, not control.
- I practice recovery as maintenance, not punishment.
- I keep my north in sight.

Island Vows

- My shores are open; my borders are true.
- I welcome wonder; I protect the tide.
- Guests are invited; weather is named.
- I leave the beach better than I found it.

Peninsula Vows

- I articulate seasons of closeness.
- I build bridges that lift, not tolls that trap.
- I schedule replenish days after shared time.

Mountain Top/Bottom Vows

- Top: I bring oxygen (sleep, food, water) to wisdom.
- Base: I climb by window, not mood.
- Both: I descend before bravado arrives.

River Vows

- I flow with banks.
- I name speed and depth before entering.
- I rest in pools; I do not promise rapids to prove love.

Forest Vows

- I mark the path for returns.
- I invite light on purpose.
- I tell the truth even when it echoes.

City Vows

- Comments ≠ summons; office hours protect presence.
- I ask, *"What decision are we making?"* before meetings.
- I walk my north line at dusk.

Write your vows here (3–7 lines):

1. _____
2. _____
3. _____
4. _____
5. _____
6. _____
7. _____

[Handwritten Affirmation: I am generous within form.]

III. Edgework & Cadence (Pace protects heat)

A. Edge Map (current season)

- Green (welcome): _____
- Yellow (curious, slow): _____
- Red (no): _____

B. Weekly Cadence

- Two Embers (5–10 min): _____ /
  _____
- One Kindling (≤1 hr): _____
- One Fire (≤3 hrs): _____

Signal Lexicon (choose 3–5 cues)

- One tap = slow the pace
- Two taps = pause; breath check
- Open palm = capacity check (say your color)
- Small nod with eye contact = I'm here
- Hand to chest once = I need a minute, stay close
  Custom: _____

  [Handwritten Affirmation: Cadence protects desire.]

IV. Symbols & North (Choose your anchors)

Circle or draw: Phoenix (thrust) · Lotus (ballast) · Spiral (returns) · Open Palm (receive/release) · Vesica Piscis(overlap / dignity) · First-Quarter Moon (in-process) · Jupiter (expansion with form) · Sagittarius Arrow (aim).

- My north (word or image): _____
- My altar (shelf, window, desk): _____

- My gesture (on stage/under stress): _____
- My object (stone/coin) lives: _____

[Handwritten Affirmation: Aim before I move.]

V. Your Landing Poem (Weave what you love)

Choose one frame (you can do more later). Insert your words. Whisper it once after writing.

A) Tide Poem (Island/River/Sea)
I arrive at the water named [_____].
It speaks [sound/verb] against a shore that [truth].
I offer [vow]; I refuse [red edge].
If the tide rises, I will [recovery plan].
I leave [gift] for the morning that finds me.

B) Slope Poem (Mountain/Desert)
There is air here thin enough for [clarity].
I carry [floor habit] like rope.
I ascend until [signal], then descend with [kindness].
I refuse [bravado/performance].
I promise [cadence] to the ground that holds me.

C) Canopy Poem (Forest/City/Continent)
Under [structure] I practice [ritual].
The path returns where [symbol] marks the bend.
I speak [one exact sentence] before I act.
I let [light/source] through on purpose.
I exit [time] and return with [small offering].

Optional insert lines from your history (poems, memories, prayer):
— *Line I keep:* _____
— *Line I release:* _____

    [Handwritten Affirmation: Small kept promises, sacred life.]

VI. Two Notes (public & private)

Public Note (3 sentences max; post someday, or don't):

_____

_____

Private Note (to yourself; read before sleep):

_____

_____

    [Handwritten Affirmation: I witness without erasing.]

VII. Three Windows (24h / 7d / 30d)

Within 24 hours — One ember you will do: _____

Within 7 days — One kindling you will schedule: _____

Within 30 days — One fire you will honor: _____

Micro-scripts (use/adapt):

- "I'm keeping what holds me. Thursday 6–7 works."
- "Capacity check: yellow. I want closeness, low volume."
- "I won't do midnight decisions. Morning call?"
- *Spanish:* "Respeto mi norte. Podemos hablar mañana a las 10."

VIII. Reverence Inventory (credit your light)

Name three influences—people/places/practices—you don't own but that steadied your hands.

1. _____ — *What they gave me:* _____
2. _____ — *What they gave me:* _____
3. _____ — *What they gave me:* _____

Write a one-line benediction for each:
— *For* ___: _____
— *For* ___: _____
— *For* ___: _____

[Handwritten Affirmation: Continue, but with thanks.]

IX. Landing Ceremony (5 minutes, anytime)

1. Stand. One hand heart, one belly. Breath 4–4–6 × 4.
2. Touch water (bowl). Speak your terrain aloud.
3. Place coin/stone where your altar lives.
4. Read your vows once, steady.
5. Read your poem once, softer.
6. Bow a little. Walk your corridor (door→desk, sink→bed).

7. Exit on time.

X. If and When (the bridge forward)

If alignment is real—tonight or ten years from now—your paths and fires will test themselves. You will not force ignition; you will arrive prepared: capacity named, cadence agreed, dignity intact. You will meet others at the edge of a well-kept field or a well-kept shore. Ember first. Kindling next. Fire by design. If the mountain rumbles, you will not pretend it can't. You will keep your go-bag ready, bless the view you chose, and leave on time.

The point is not to finish. The point is to return with reverence—and to live your chosen geography with an open palm. When you turn the page, there may be an island. There may be a continent. There may be a woman placing two fingers in your open hand. There will be you.

> [Handwritten Affirmation: I land here. I live here. I keep going.]

Ritual • Benediction of the Reader (3 minutes)

Whisper:

- *I return to floor.*
- *I return to form.*
- *I return to favor.*
  Then: *I choose my terrain, and it chooses me back.*

Breath 4–4–6 × 3. Close the book gently.

Journal Prompts (for any season)

- What terrain did I choose and why—today?
- Which vow kept my heat honest this week?
- Where did cadence save my desire from spectacle?
- What five bright specks proved my life back to me?
- Finish: *Dignity is where my discipline and my desire shake hands when...*

Chapter 13 - Island & Infinity

Chapter 13 — Island & Infinity *(your "final," for now...)*

Epigraph
I choose the view, knowing the mountain.

I want my own island. Not a deed—an orientation. A place like Water Island in the Caribbean, where people choose coastline with their eyes open, where risk is part of the air and joy doesn't apologize. The same way some live under Vesuvius and call it home—accepting what could be to value the sky they do have. I want that kind of choosing.

Everything that crosses my shore—people, moments, enter-actions— adds to the map: my landscape, my access, my capacity, my desire, my discipline. Women—oh, how I love the many kinds of them. I love to collect and tend: nourish, protect, and allow—free within their capacity inside mine. No cages; only coves. When it's aligned, we chart. When it isn't, we wave from the pier and keep the tide clean.

Some relationships arrived like the grocery-store bouquet—premade, plastic sleeve, the idea of intention. I added baby's breath and ribbon to suggest thought, then learned that suggestion isn't soil. Some were florist flowers—rooted, chosen with care by hands that asked my purpose (*for my ninety-six-year-old grandmother*) and responded with reverence because humanity recognizes itself. Others, I picked wild—on a random path, destination undecided, delighting in the unruly of it. Some encounters were only a whiff—a scent that sparked clarity: yes, boundary; yes, edge—and we both knew.

As I allow freeness, I cannot forsake my freedom. Not again. Not by drifting from discipline, skipping cadence, leaving the shore unguarded.

My island needs a lighthouse and a schedule: grounded, clear, unwavering. That's how visitors remain guests and not weather.

I enjoy beautiful things. I enjoy beautiful, authentic moments and people. I learn from their worlds, soak their essence—especially that of a woman, a particular woman. I accept my soft spot for those who echo the women who raised and ringed me—mother, sister, aunties, girlfriends—their examples beacons I could not read until I could. That root makes my intention permanent: honesty, protection, preservation. For this to grow into what I desire and love, I must stay forever present in my world.

It's me. The island is me.

> [Handwritten Affirmation: I keep my shores open and my edges true.]

The Island Vows

- Freedom with form. Your freedom doesn't end mine; our edges bless the waterline.
- Cadence over chaos. Ember → kindling → agreed fire; arrivals and exits on time.
- Tend what you collect. If I invite it, I water it—or I release it cleanly.
- Clean heat. Phoenix for thrust, Lotus for ballast. No smoke shows.
- Honor the scent. When essence speaks—yes, boundary; yes, desire—answer without costume.
- Reverence for roots. Grandmothers, mothers, aunties—light I don't own, only inherit.
- Leave the beach better. If we share a cove, we depart without litter—no stories left burning.

[Handwritten Affirmation: I welcome wonder. I protect the tide.]

If alignment is real—tonight or ten years from now—paths and fires will meet themselves. We won't force ignition; we'll arrive prepared: capacity named, cadence agreed, dignity intact. Two practiced flames at the edge of a well-kept field, then shore. Ember first. Kindling next. Fire by design. And if the mountain rumbles? We do not pretend it can't. We keep our go-bags ready, bless the view we chose, and leave on time.

I walk the perimeter once—Open Palm to the water, Vesica to the overlap, Spiral for the returns that rise. The moon lays its coin on the channel and the island answers with a steady light.

I enjoy beautiful things. I enjoy people who are not performances. I enjoy being the steward of where I stand. To keep any of it true, I bow to the floors that hold me—breath, movement, north—and to the favor that meets me when I keep them.

It's me. It has always been me.

[Handwritten Affirmation: I am shore, and I am ship.]

The End... until.

The Island Accord - Guest Edition

The Island Accord — Guest Edition

Welcome to the island—shores open and edges true. This guide tells you exactly how to land, stay, and play here so we can keep warmth without mess.

Cadence (Weekly, Not Daily)

Cadence is WEEKLY, not daily.
 - The rhythm is **2 embers + 1 kindling + 1 fire (max)** **per person, per week**—that's up to **4 hang windows** total.
 - Most days we won't hang; we keep a daily **10–15 min text check-in window** for warmth and logistics.
 - We can always do **less**. We only do more after a seasonal review.

What counts

Embers (5–30 min) — walk, tea sit, poem aloud, short voice-note swap, breath together, playlist + one listen, quick kitchen dance, 20-min co-work.
 Kindling (45–90 min) — simple cook-and-eat, gallery/bookstore, porch talk, class, grocery + one-dish, park loop.
 Fire (≤3 hours) — concert/event + debrief, short day trip, intimacy window with consent, creative session with plan.

Scheduling

How we schedule
 - We'll propose times on **Sundays** for the week (or say "quiet week").
 - **One window per day** max; **buffer days** around a fire.
 - **Ad-hoc** hangs are OK when both are **Green** and with **2 hours notice**.
 - If life shifts, we reschedule once with grace; more than once = pause.

Daily Text Window

We keep one **10–15 minute** text window daily (e.g., 5:00–5:15 p.m.). Outside it, replies are welcome **not expected**.

C•A•B Every Time

Capacity (G/Y/R) • **Aim** (1 sentence) • **Boundary** (1 sentence).
 Example: "Capacity **yellow**; Aim: tea and decompress, 20 minutes; Boundary: phones down."

No Triangulation

We do not route feelings or conflicts through third parties. No subtweets, no screenshot sharing without consent, no friend-couriers. Instead: direct talk, personal processing with a pro, or a one-time logistics mediator if both agree.

Agreement to Land

By stepping onto the dock, you agree to keep cadence, use C•A•B, honor boundaries (two bends end the season), and choose direct channels over triangles. My vow to you: I keep my floors, I don't wear costumes, and I leave the beach better.

The Becoming

The Becoming

There comes a moment when reflection no longer hurts—when it hums.
When you realize every loss was a lesson, every love a mirror, every
silence a teacher.
And suddenly, you are no longer chasing healing—you are living it.

This is *The Becoming.*
The slow and sacred unfolding of a life that finally feels like yours.
The recognition that peace is not found—it is remembered.
It lives beneath the noise, beneath the performance, beneath the layers
we shed in pursuit of self.

I used to believe arrival meant perfection.
Now I understand that becoming has no finish line—only moments of
clarity, glimpses of divinity,
and the quiet courage to begin again.
To walk differently.
To love differently.
To live honestly.

What I know now is simple:
Becoming isn't about becoming more.
It's about becoming true.
About reclaiming what has always been sacred within you.

So I close this book the way I now rise each morning—
not as the man I was yesterday,
but as the one I am ready to meet today.

—*L.E.S.Jr.*

About the Author

About The Author

Lawrence "Law" Sturdivant Jr, currently known as "Laurion- Asahn" is a memoirist, keynote speaker, artist, credited actor and corporate professional of many years whose work centers on recovery as maintenance and desire without costumes. Born of two unique beings, his path was clear early on: cultivate presence, keep clean edges, and build forms that let love move. Raised in Waterbury, Connecticut, he writes about endings that become architectures—breath as method, boundaries as mercy, cadence as protection.

A lover of life and beauty—of discipline and flow—Law designs practices people can actually use: the Island Accord (Capacity • Aim • Boundary), scaled contact windows (embers • kindling • fire), and seasonal councils that protect growth. Before and alongside his creative work, he spent many years in corporate environments translating clarity and cadence into teams and systems; he is both master and student, always learning and refining. A graduate of the University of Connecticut (UConn), he delivers keynotes, workshops, and studio-style residencies for communities, schools, and organizations seeking clarity, repair, and ritual without pretense.

When he isn't writing or speaking, he's sketching, walking shoreline loops, or helping others chart their own landings. Find resources and practice guides at lawsturdivantjr.com.

Reader's Key

Esoteric Glossary

This book uses a few recurring themes and "inner markers" to help you track the emotional direction of a passage. They are not icons or QR cues—just shorthand for the kind of moment you're in.

- Open Palm — Release/receive; boundary clarity; consent and capacity.
- Overlap *(formerly "Vesica Piscis")* — Where two truths meet; dignity in the middle.
- Phoenix — Clean heat; engineered rising; transformation without residue.
- Lotus — Ballast; grace after honest mess; staying afloat through the muck.
- Spiral — Returning at a higher level; iteration with kindness.
- Ember / Kindling / Fire — Scaled contact windows: 5–30 min / 45–90 min / ≤3 hrs.
- First-Quarter — Mid-cycle becoming; a natural scene break.
- Jupiter — Expansion with form; growth that stays disciplined.
- Arrow *(formerly "Sagittarius Arrow")* — Aim before movement; exit on time.

Owner's Manual "Season & Safety" Appendix

Owner's Manual *"Season & Safety"* appendix

1) What is a "season"?

Default: a 13-week container (your *Season Loom*) with:

- Week 7 = Fallow (lighter load; still keep floors)
- Week 13 = Harvest (review, upgrade one inch)
- Council at the end (2 hours: keep / cut / upgrade / release)

New connections: treat the first 4 weeks as the Dock Micro-Season (embers only; calibration, not acceleration).

Why: Seasons prevent drift and drama. You promise *cadence*, not forever. Rhythm is the agreement.

---

2) Is cadence based on "offense level"?

Cadence is weekly by design (2 embers + 1 kindling + 1 fire, max). Adjust access using this simple matrix:

Offense & Repair Matrix

- Severity (S): *S1 minor miss → S2 misattunement → S3 harm / breach*
- Frequency (F): *first time → repeated → patterned*
- Repair (R): *owns + repairs → minimizes → refuses*

Response ladder

- S1/F1/R+ → Redirect (name it; keep cadence)
- S1–2/repeat or R± → Repair (48-hr window) + reduce access one ring
- S2–3/repeat or R- → Pause for rest of season (or a full season)
- S3 or any non-consent / safety breach → End (clean exit)

---

3) Final boundaries (deal breakers)

These end the season immediately (no debate, clean exit).

Non-consent / coercion / cruelty / violence — *reef strike; the harbor must close for safety.*

1. Chronic lying / double-life — *false charts sink boats.*
2. Triangulation with intent (smearing, ally-recruiting, leaks) — *erosion of the coast.*
3. Privacy violations (screenshots, recordings, sharing intimacies without consent) — *sanctuary destroyed.*
4. Repeated boundary bending after clear naming — *shoreline collapse.*
5. Health-risk disregard (sexual health, substance risk around me/children) — *toxic spill in the water.*
6. Contempt, bigotry, humiliation — *salting the soil.*
7. Breach of declared structure (e.g., cheating in an exclusive frame) — *lighthouse goes dark.*

   Two bends of any *non-deal-breaker* boundary in one season = automatic pause for the rest of the season.

---

4) "Unconditional love" vs access

- Love can be unconditional as a *stance.*
- Access is always conditional—on behavior, capacity, cadence, and repair.

  Mantra: *Love is a stance; access is a schedule.*

When *unconditional love* is used to bypass harm, you get erosion. When it's paired with clear access rules, you get habitat.

5) "Are these inquiries fear that I will let go?"

Sometimes. Use this clarity check:

Fear or Knowing? (3 questions)

1. *Is my body calm after I name the boundary?* (calm = knowing; spin = fear)
2. *Is the request about access (present behavior) or worth (identity)?* (access = clean; worth talk = fear)
3. *If I had to enforce this for a stranger, would I?* (yes = knowing)

If it's fear of loss, breathe + witness. If it's knowing, act now at the smallest honest scale.

6) Why this structure exists

To remove the need for detachment theater and block fake "support". Form catches love so love doesn't need to perform. Honesty the first time is cheaper than repair later.

Three-Sentence Truth (any moment)

1. Observation: "When X happened..."
2. Meaning: "...I felt Y because Z matters to me."
3. Request / Boundary: "I need A. Without it, I'll do B."

---

7) C•A•B made unmistakable

- Capacity (G/Y/R) — Green = resourced; Yellow = limited/quiet pace; Red = rest/logistics only.
- Aim (1 sentence) — purpose for *this* window.
- Boundary (1 sentence) — condition that keeps both safe.
  Script: "Capacity yellow. Aim: tea and decompress, 20 minutes. Boundary: phones down."

---

8) The Jungian arc you're naming (without cosplay)

From the porous Empath (over-merging, rescuing) to Sovereignty (compassion with edges).

Sovereignty = Presence + Preference + Protection

- Presence: witness without fusing (Mirror Ledger, 3 minutes).
- Preference: name what you want without apology (Aim).
- Protection: enforce the boundary you named (Protection ≠ punishment; it's maintenance).

Mantra: *I move on desire with NO costumes. I keep my floors when love gets loud.*

Tiny cards you can carry (and share)

Season Card

- 13 weeks. Week 7 fallow. Week 13 harvest. Council → keep/cut/upgrade/release.

Access Card

- Weekly max: 2 embers • 1 kindling • 1 fire (most days = no hang).
- Daily: one 10–15 min text window. Replies welcome, not expected.

Exit Card

- Departure Three: what I received • what boundary was honored • one sentence to carry.
- Ends = courtesy, not trial. 30 days no contact unless logistics.

Deal-Breaker Card

- Non-consent, cruelty/violence, chronic lying, triangulation, privacy violations, repeated boundary bending, health-risk disregard, contempt/bigotry, agreed-frame breach.

Publishing Details Section
(for bottom layout)

Publishing Details Section

ISBNs:

Ebook: 979-8-993-5035-9-2

Paperback: 979-8-218-64062-0

Audiobook: 979-8-993-5035-8-5

Published by Sovereign Crowns Creative House Publishing LLC

A subsidiary of Lawrence E. Sturdivant Jr LLC

New Britain, CT

www.LawSturdivantJr.com | @LawSturdivantJr

www.ingramcontent.com/pod-product-compliance
Lightning Source LLC
Chambersburg PA
CBHW020421130626
46549CB00006B/2683